Contents

Publisher & Editor-in-Chief: **Thomas H.W. Emanuel** • Executive Editor: **Edward R. Ricciuti** • Assistant Editor: **Lou Gianfriddo** • Design: **JAT Associates** • Photography Director: **Stephen H. Taylor** •Staff Photographer: **Tom Buchanan** • Production: **Georgette McClure** • Photo Editors: **Marybeth Cavanagh, Donna Schmerzler** • Copy Editor: **Midge Bacon** • Typesetting Manager: **Linda L. Nishball** • Puzzles: **Larry Humber**

Published by Grandreams Limited, Jadwin House, 205/211 Kentish Town Road, London, NW5 2JU
Printed in Italy. ISBN 1-85830-142-4

WWF WrestleMania X

TEN YEARS IN THE MAKING!

It all began on March 31, 1985, at New York's Madison Square Garden. It was billed as the wrestling extravaganza of the century. From Rowdy Roddy Piper to Andre the Giant, the card read like a Who's Who of Professional Wrestling. Everybody who was anybody was there. At the time, nobody realized the piece of history that was about to take place. No one ever thought that a decade later the World Wrestling Federation would be celebrating the birthday of the spectacular called *WrestleMania*. But here they were! Ten years in the making on March 20, 1994, history rewrote itself as the world witnessed *WrestleMania* X from the place where it all began, Madison Square Garden. This event has become the pinnacle of the wrestling year.

World Wrestling Federation Women's Champion Alundra Blayze successfully defended her belt against a ruthless Leilani Kai. Earlier in the event, Owen Hart beat brother Bret in a preliminary championship bout shocker.

It was payback day for Crush, when the Macho Man Randy Savage evened the score in a falls-count-anywhere match, but the highlight of the evening came when Bret "Hit Man" Hart defeated Yokozuna, thus becoming two-time World Wrestling Federation Champion.

Two highlights from the spectacle were the mixed tag team match, in which Bam Bam Bigelow and Luna Vachon defeated Doink and Dink, and the grueling Ladder Match in which the Bad Guy Razor Ramon successfully defended his Intercontinental Title against the Heartbreak Kid Shawn Michaels.

Bret Hit Man

Bret "Hit Man" Hart lost the World Wrestling Federation Title to Yokozuna at *WrestleMania IX*, largely due to interference by Yoko's manager, Mr. Fuji. However, he didn't brood over it. He battled his way to becoming King of the Ring and the 1993 Federation Superstar of the Year.

At the *Royal Rumble*'s battle royal, Bret and Lex Luger, the last two men in the ring, went out simultaneously. That made them both eligible for a shot at Yokozuna's title at *WrestleMania X*. Then Bret would go against the winner of that match—all on the same night. Luger lost to Yokozuna by disqualification. However, Bret triumphed, taking the title. He became the first man ever to hold all three titles twice.

Hart*

Lex Luger*

On July 4, Lex Luger showed up on the deck of the aircraft carrier *USS Intrepid* in New York City to slam Yokozuna, the huge World Wrestling Champion, who was laughing at American athletes who failed in trying to bodyslam him.

SummerSlam. Luger beats Yokozuna. But no title for Luger because he won by a count-out after he knocked Yokozuna cold and out of the ring.

The winner of the 30-man battle royal at the *Royal Rumble* would contend for Yoko's belt at *WrestleMania X*. Lex and Bret "Hit Man" Hart were co-winners. A coin toss determined Lex would first wrestle the Japanese giant; then the winner of that match would face Bret for the title.

Lex had Yokozuna beaten, but Mr. Perfect disqualified Luger, an act which led to bad blood between them.

Yokozuna*

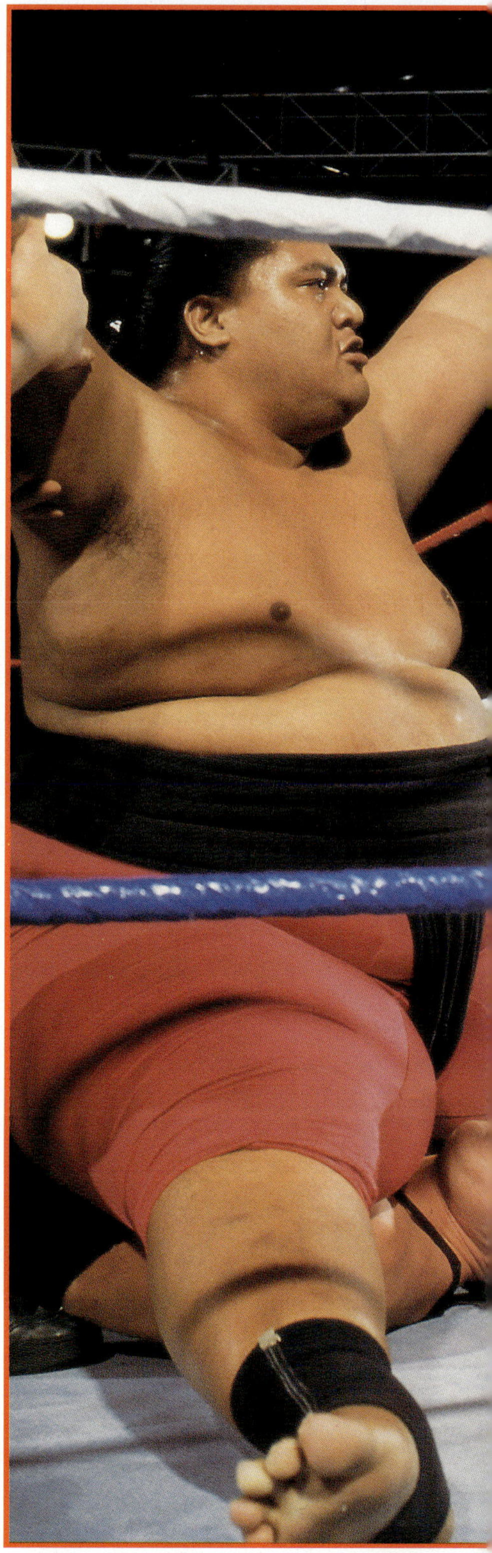

Yokozuna took the World Wrestling Federation Title from Bret "Hit Man" Hart at *WrestleMania IX*. Moments later, Yoko challenged Hulk Hogan to wrestle him then and there. Hulk accepted and got the title, but Yoko took it back a short time later.

At the *Royal Rumble*, Yokozuna was faced by the Undertaker in a Coffin Match. The winner would be the man who stuffed his opponent into a coffin and closed it. The match had no other rules.

The Undertaker clobbered Yoko unconscious and put him in the coffin. Before he could shut the lid, though, the Undertaker was attacked by almost a dozen of Yoko's allies. Thus, Yokozuna survived the match.

At *WrestleMania X* Yokozuna met both Lex Luger and Bret Hart, one right after the other, for the Championship Belt. He beat Luger by a count-out but, after an exhausting match, lost to Hart.

No Rest For The Undertaker

Someone is going around pretending to be the Undertaker. The real Undertaker is shown at the top right of this page; the imposter, at the bottom left. There are 12 differences between the two of them. How many can you come up with?

1. ______________________
2. ______________________
3. ______________________
4. ______________________
5. ______________________
6. ______________________
7. ______________________
8. ______________________
9. ______________________
10. ______________________
11. ______________________
12. ______________________

Did you find all twelve differences? Be sure and turn to page 46 to compare your answers and see how well you know the real Undertaker.

Doink* & Dink*

Doink the Clown demonstrated his mastery of technical skills—as well as jokes and tricks—by beating the huge Crush at *WrestleMania IX*. It seems that Doink continually gets mixed up with the meanest behemoths he can find in the World Wrestling Federation. He succeeded in making a fool out of Bam Bam Bigelow and his main squeeze, Luna Vachon, outside the ring and stood up to him inside it. Doink found a sidekick, his little double, Dink.

They went up against Bigelow and Luna during *WrestleMania X* and, after a violent battle, lost.

Razor Ramon*

Razor Ramon has always loved gold. That's why he wears so much of it around his neck. But no gold is more treasured by Razor than that which he first strapped around his waist in the autumn—the World Wrestling Federation Intercontinental Belt.

Razor's road to the title started when Federation President Jack Tunney took it away from Shawn Michaels for not defending it often enough. A battle royal was scheduled, with the last two men in the ring to contend for the vacant title. The final two were Razor and the Model Rick Martel. A week later, they fought for the big prize. Razor prevailed, then successfully defended the title against Shawn Michaels at *WrestleMania X*.

Adam Bomb*

Adam Bomb has exploded upon the World Wrestling Federation with megaton force. The huge brute with the glowing eyes, who comes from Three Mile Island, has obliterated the competition with ease, smashing his way to victory with blows such as bone-rattling clotheslines and forearms.

Managed by Johnny Polo, Adam Bomb is confident that he will soon score in a big way within the Federation ring.

"The World Wrestling Federation has changed forever now that I have arrived," booms Adam Bomb. "I bring absolute destruction to my foes, one they cannot avoid. Destruction that will blast them into nothingness. Adam Bomb will rule the entire World Wrestling Federation."

Macho Man

Randy Savage*

You just don't step on Superman's cape. And you just don't turn on Macho Man Randy Savage, Pearl Harbor him, then beat him with the aid of your monstrous new ally, World Wrestling Federation Champion Yokozuna. Crush found that out in November.

Soon after his attack, Savage was commentating at ringside during *Monday Night Raw*. Crush showed up to wrestle but never made it to the ring. As he made his way down the aisle, Savage erupted from the announcers' table and tore into Crush. Savage was on Crush like glue. The fight spilled into the dressing room, then the street. When the match was over, Crush was a hurting puppy. He hurt even more after Macho Man Savage whipped him very convincingly at *WrestleMania X*.

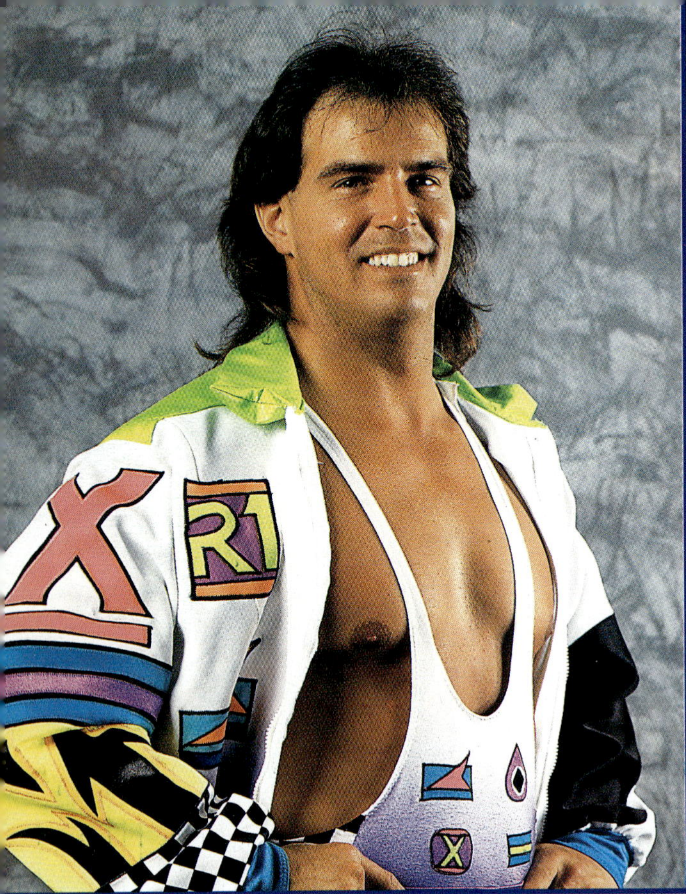

“NEW

There is a new breed of athlete in the World Wrestling Federation. They're big, they're fast, but most of all, they're hungry. So everyone in the squared circle should be warned:

KIDS"...

They are definitely here to stay!

Every so often, a newcomer to the World Wrestling Federation surprises fans by being a quick achiever. But nobody has ever done it like the 1-2-3 Kid. When the Kid showed up, people wondered. After all, among the big, muscular men of the Federation, he looked, well, like a kid. His super athletic abilities were not evident at first when he was squashed repeatedly by opponents. But then he pulled off the big shocker. He beat Razor Ramon. And the Kid was on his way. He took on the big guys and notched win after win, even—in partnership with Marty Jannetty—holding the Tag Team Title, although briefly. Now the Kid can stand amongst the Federation's giants.

From out of the Southland and the car racing circuit came Sparky Plugg, revving up his engine in a new kind of competition. Automobile racer Plugg has vowed that he will speed to the very top of the Federation's singles ranks.

Jeff Jarrett, Double J, left Music City—Nashville, Tennessee—to try his luck in the Federation. Double J blamed the Nashville music establishment for not accepting him. He promised that he would become the greatest superstar in the Federation and that then the music industry would come begging.

IN THI

Another lethal newcomer to the Federation is Kwang, a mysterious ninja warrior who blends the mystic oriental fighting arts with wrestling techniques. This masked assassin is a frightening opponent because he understands methods of fighting known only to the secret cult of the ninjas. Every time he steps into the ring, Kwang unleashes a new weapon of destruction. No one knows what to expect from him next.

A strange, ghostly new entrant into the Federation is MVP, who appears to have come from Big League baseball. However, the real identity of MVP is not known. Nor is it known whether he has the ability to score in the wrestling ring.

Duke Dumpster Droesè burst onto the scene in the spring and is proving himself a force to be reckoned with. The Federation's fans have already taken this good-natured giant into their hearts.

E RING

Crush*

Crush has displayed his true colors. Injured, he retired to his beaufiful native Hawaiian Islands to recover. Once there, he grew embittered. "Nobody cared about me," he bitterly claimed. "Not the fans, especially my so-called friend Macho Man Randy Savage."

Revealing that he was partially Japanese, Crush scorned America and allied himself with mighty Yokozuna and his manager, Mr. Fuji. They viciously ambushed Savage and severely beat him. But you just don't mess with Randy Savage that way. He returned the favor by pounding Crush. Crush then vowed revenge against the Macho Man.

At *WrestleMania X* they battled in a match where the rules allowed them to fight in and out of the ring. The fray was vicious, the action fast and furious, but in the end Savage was the victor and prevailed.

Undertaker*

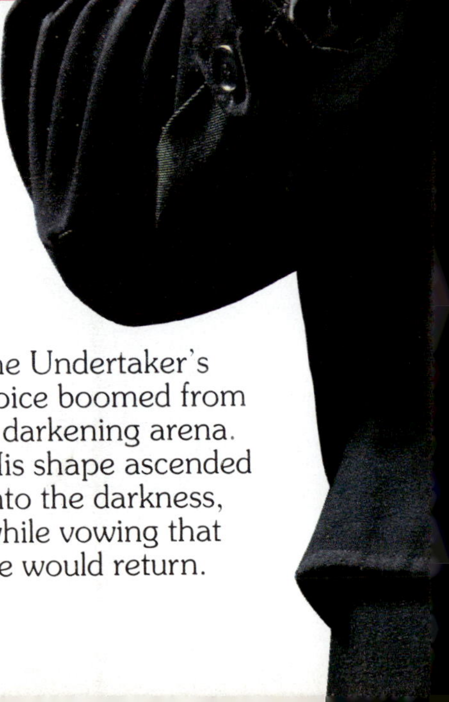

The Undertaker faced Yokozuna at the *Royal Rumble* for the World Wrestling Federation Title. There were no rules except that the man who stuffed his opponent into a coffin and shut the lid would win.

Eventually, the two men collided and collapsed. But the Undertaker rose and put an unconscious Yoko in the coffin. Before he could close the lid, the Untertaker was assailed by a dozen brutes, including Crush, Diesel and Tenryu. They beat him ferociously, but he resisted through the power of the funeral urn carried by his manager, Paul Bearer. That is, until a recovered Yokozuna smashed the urn over the Reaper's skull. When Undertaker's power escaped the urn in the form of ghostly green smoke, he faded and was enclosed in the coffin.

As Yoko and his allies wheeled away the coffin, the Undertaker's voice boomed from a darkening arena. His shape ascended into the darkness, while vowing that he would return.

Diesel*

After bodyguarding Shawn Michaels, this 7-foot-tall thug decided to try his luck in the ring on his own. Using his brutal street-fighting tactics, plus his immense height, Diesel rolled over the competition like—you guessed it—a diesel locomotive.

Diesel makes no bones about his wrestling style. "I like to beat on people. I'm big enough to do it. So I don't have to use any fancy moves. I just look down on the punks I wrestle and smash them to a pulp."

GAMES

City Search

A number of major American cities have been the sites of one or more of the Federation's big events—*WrestleMania, SummerSlam,* the *Survivor Series* and the *Royal Rumble*. Eleven of those cities are hidden in the maze of letters. They are ATLANTIC CITY, BOSTON, CHICAGO, HOUSTON, INDIANAPOLIS, LAS VEGAS, LOS ANGELES, MIAMI, NEW YORK, ORLANDO and PHILADELPHIA. All the cities read either across or down, though some are backward. Many of the cities overlap. Take the overlapping letters and rearrange them to come up with the name of the European capital that was the site of *SummerSlam '92*. Good luck!

C	H	I	C	A	G	O	M	O	D	N	A	L	R	O
M	F	X	J	S	S	Q	T	Y	G	N	D	A	H	R
C	V	B	N	M	I	B	J	L	L	K	F	S	W	Q
P	L	C	B	Y	N	N	R	U	J	P	W	V	D	G
P	H	I	L	A	D	E	L	P	H	I	A	E	N	J
Q	W	V	N	Y	I	F	Q	B	C	M	K	G	P	T
V	T	H	C	S	A	W	L	N	T	K	D	A	G	X
S	E	L	E	G	N	A	S	O	L	Y	S	S	D	H
R	P	J	R	L	A	C	V	T	W	K	H	P	M	X
T	W	S	M	Z	P	H	N	S	V	R	L	L	I	V
H	O	U	S	T	O	N	Q	O	B	O	S	Y	A	D
N	F	L	T	P	L	R	G	B	H	Y	J	R	M	Q
B	M	P	S	W	I	T	J	X	R	W	T	B	I	L
A	Z	C	D	G	S	Z	P	H	Q	E	S	M	D	C
M	Y	B	Y	T	I	C	C	I	T	N	A	L	T	A

TAG TEAMS

The Smoking Gunns...Men On A Mission...The Quebecers and more. Non-stop team action is twice the excitement and twice the fun!

The World Wrestling Federation Tag Team Title has changed hands several times during this year. The most recent changes focused on the Quebecers, Jacques and Pierre, managed by Johnny Polo. They stripped the title from the Steiner Brothers in a shocker. Following their win, Jacques and Pierre became more overbearing than ever. They smirked and posed, basking in the warm glow of praise from the sleazy Polo. They also used every sneaky trick they could think of to keep their belts from challengers. Briefly, they lost the title to the 1-2-3 Kid and Marty Jannetty, but within a matter of only days retrieved it.

The Quebecers went into *WrestleMania X* with the gold. Their opponents were rappers Men on a Mission (M.O.M.), Mo and the 500-pound-plus Mabel. Managed by Oscar, the Men went on a rampage against the Quebecers, pounding them from pillar to post. The Quebecers appeared finished, to the delight of most fans. However, they used a typical dirty trick to keep the belts. They allowed themselves to be counted out, and titles cannot change hands that way. Less than two months later, however, Jacques and Pierre ran out of time. They faced the Head Shrinkers, who acted as if they wanted to eat them alive. They didn't, but the Shrinkers won the match and the title.

In other tag team action, Texans Billy and Bart Gunn—the Smoking Gunns—continued to provide plenty of excitement for fans. Observers believe that, with more seasoning in the ring, these two young cowboys will continue to rise through the ranks of Federation tag team duos. "We are more than willing to pay our dues," says Billy. "That's the way to get ahead in the World Wrestling Federation."

"Right, Billy," adds Bart. "You just don't get to be a top hand in this outfit without lots of hard work."

The Bushwhackers, cousins Luke and Butch, delighted hordes of fans with their wild and woolly antics—and their rugged tactics in the ring. Loyal followers simply can't wait to see the zany things the Bushwhackers will do next. Whatever it is, their foes are bound to be surprised!

Blayze*

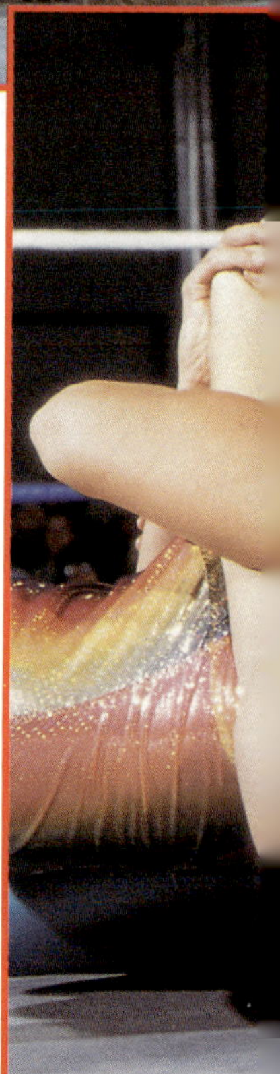

The year 1993 marked the exciting return of the Women's Division to the ranks of the World Wrestling Federation, with the title being won by Alundra Blayze.

Alundra says she wants to be a role model for all women in the 1990s, encouraging them to be the best they can be. She has always been. Alundra learned martial arts in Japan while competing in wrestling there. She can bench-press almost 245 pounds and squat close to 280. Alundra is also an expert scuba diver and has been in the water with sharks.

"My goal is to be the best female athlete in the world," she said. Alundra took a major step toward achieving that goal at *WrestleMania X* by defeating challenger Leilani Kai.

GAMES

*WrestleMania**: Which One Was It?

WrestleMania recently celebrated its 10th anniversary. How much do you remember about that fabulous first decade? Each of the following passages describes one of the 10 *WrestleManias*. It's up to you to fill in the appropriate numbers.

- *WrestleMania* is normally a one-arena affair, with the exception of ***WrestleMania*** ____, which took place in three different arenas in three different time zones.

- Fans were treated to a dual main event at ***WrestleMania*** ____, in which a couple of titles changed hands.

- ***WrestleMania*** ____ wasn't one to remember for Macho Man Randy Savage, who lost his Federation Title in an explosion of Mega-Powers.

- One of the zaniest matches in Federation history took place at ***WrestleMania*** ____. It involved two of the Federation's big men, Hillbilly Jim and King Kong Bundy, and a handful of midgets.

- It was fitting that ***WrestleMania*** ____ took place at the same venue as the inaugural *WrestleMania*.

- *WrestleMania* was Born in the USA, and it remained there until ***WrestleMania*** ____, when it played before a packed house at SkyDome in Toronto, Canada.

- Rocker Cyndi Lauper and late pianist Liberace were just two of the celebrities who played a part in ***WrestleMania*** ____, setting the stage for other big-name entertainers to get involved.

- *WrestleMania* went outdoors for the first time at ***WrestleMania*** ____, which was dubbed "The World's Largest Toga Party."

- It was tournament time at ***WrestleMania*** ____, in which Savage grabbed the Federation Title for the first time.

- With the Gulf War already won, the world turned its attention to ***WrestleMania*** ____, at which American turncoat Sgt. Slaughter got his comeuppance. Sadly, it was Andre the Giant's last hurrah.

Tatanka*

Tatanka has had good luck and bad luck. At *WrestleMania IX*, he took on then-Intercontinental Champion Shawn Michaels and gave him a lesson in wrestling skills and courage. Tatanka took the duke. But he did not take the belt from the Heartbreak Kid. Why? Because the win was by a count-out, and a title doesn't change hands that way.

Next, Tatanka got into it with Bam Bam Bigelow. And the Native American won out. At *Summer-Slam*, after Tatanka's tag partners the Smoking Gunns had been ousted, he survived an assault from Bigelow and the Head Shrinkers and emerged victorious.

Shawn

For Shawn Michaels, the past year was a case of sour grapes. After Michaels defeated Mr. Perfect at *SummerSlam* via a count-out, he became even cockier than usual. Too big for his britches, Michaels decided to defend

Michaels*

his Intercontinental Title only when he felt like it.

Eventually, Tunney's patience ran out, and he stripped Michaels of the title, which ended up with Razor Ramon. Furious, Michaels produced his old belt and declared himself the true champion. Jack Tunney would have none of it and told Michaels he would have to go after Razor and take back his title the old-fashioned way, by wrestling for it. He tried at *WrestleMania X*, but failed.

Bam Bam*

In some ways, the past year has been frustrating for Bam Bam Bigelow and his main squeeze, Luna Vachon. He and his three-man tag team partners the Head Shrinkers had Tatanka all alone in the ring at *SummerSlam*—and lost. At the *Survivor Series*, he led the Head Shrinkers and Bastion Booger against the Four Doinks, who were a disguised Men on a Mission and the Bushwhackers. After his partners had been ousted, Bigelow was laid low by the Doinks. For Bam Bam Bigelow, the situation was humiliating.

However, frustration has made Bigelow even meaner, if that is possible. He and Luna put the boots to Doink and Dink while beating them mercilessly at *WrestleMania X*.

G
A
M
E
S

Says Who?

Pictured are a dozen Federation superstars, including a couple of tag teams. Alongside is a quote from each of them. But the quotes aren't in the proper order. It is up to you to match the superstars with their quotes.

1. "We're here to sink boats, not showboat."
2. "Don't think about it; do it."
3. "Rest in peace."
4. "That's the name of the game—winning at all costs."
5. "I think people relate to me."
6. "Keep laughing, keep smiling and never say never."
7. "We going to devour all the Federation's competition."
8. "What you see is what you get."
9. "It is important to try to do the right thing."
10. "When I got something going for me, I show it off."
11. "Oh yeaah!"
12. "We're on a mission."

____

____

____

____

____

____

____

____

____

____

____

____

ANSWERS

No Rest For The Undertaker

Solution: The imposter is different in these respects... he's got a feather in his hat, the hat has an abbreviated brim, he's missing a strand of hair across his face, he's got a little lump on his nose, his lip is turned up, not down, he's got a scar on his chin, much of the stubble is gone from his chin, his collar isn't as deep, he's got the intitals RIP on his chest, he's missing one of the white defining lines on the left side of his jacket, he's missing some stripes from his tie and he's only got four fingers on his left hand.

City Search

C	H	I	C	A	G	O	M	O	D	N	A	**L**	R	O
M	F	X	J	S	S	Q	T	Y	G	N	D	A	H	R
C	V	B	N	M	I	B	J	L	L	K	F	S	W	Q
P	L	C	B	Y	N	N	R	U	J	P	W	V	D	G
P	H	I	L	A	**D**	E	L	P	H	I	A	E	N	J
Q	W	V	N	Y	I	F	Q	B	C	M	K	G	P	T
V	T	H	C	S	A	W	L	N	T	K	D	A	G	X
S	E	L	E	G	**N**	A	S	**O**	L	Y	S	S	D	H
R	P	J	R	L	A	C	V	T	W	K	H	P	M	X
T	W	S	M	Z	P	H	N	S	V	R	L	L	I	V
H	O	U	S	T	**O**	N	Q	O	B	O	S	Y	A	D
N	F	L	T	P	L	R	G	B	H	Y	J	R	M	Q
B	M	P	S	W	I	T	J	X	R	W	T	B	I	L
A	Z	C	D	G	S	Z	P	H	Q	E	S	M	D	C
M	Y	B	Y	T	I	C	C	I	T	**N**	A	L	T	A

LONDON was the site of *SummerSlam '92.*

WrestleMania: Which One Was It?

Solution: From top to bottom, the *WrestleMania*s are: 2,VIII, V, III, X, VI, I, IX, IV and VII.

Says Who?

Solution: **8.** Bob Backlund, **2.** Alundra Blayze, **4.** Diesel, **6.** Doink, **7.** Head Shrinkers, **5.** 1-2-3 Kid, **9.** Lex Luger, **12.** Men on a Mission, **10.** Razor Ramon, **11.** Macho Man Randy Savage, **1.** Steiners, and **3.** Undertaker.